I0802275

TEACHING GEOGRAPHY

Roy Wilkinson

RSCP

The publisher is grateful for the encouragement and support of Robert Dulaney in making this new edition possible.

The name Waldorf really belongs only to the first school of its type, the one founded by Rudolf Steiner in Stuttgart, Germany for the children of the workers at the Waldorf-Astoria factory. It has since been adopted as the generic name of schools conducted according to Rudolf Steiner's recommendations. In place of Waldorf some establishments call themselves Rudolf Steiner schools. Others take a distinctive name and add Waldorf or Rudolf Steiner in some connection as a subtitle.

These notes are intended for the use of teachers, parents, and all those interested in the education of the child. They are based on the author's lifelong contact with Rudolf Steiner's work, including thirty years' practical experience in the classroom. In this booklet, many of the references given belong to England, since the author is a native of that country. Those living in other parts of the world may consider them somewhat remote. Nevertheless, they may serve as examples and even be of interest. The information and guidance given is general and if the references seem too local, the teacher will no doubt find equivalents.

ISBN 0-945803-56-7

Book orders may be made through Rudolf Steiner College Bookstore.
Tel. 916-961-8729, FAX 916-961-3032.

Rudolf Steiner College Press
9200 Fair Oaks Boulevard
Fair Oaks, CA 95628, USA

INTRODUCTION

The word *geography* means 'description of the earth.' There could scarcely be a definition which is more all-containing, for the earth comprises not only rocks, mountains, plains, rivers and oceans, but also plants, animals, and human beings. The atmosphere is a part of it. Although they seem a little more remote, even sun, moon and stars belong to the earth in some measure. The earth's crust contains coal, iron and a multitude of other useful materials. Human beings have found ways of traversing the land by other means than walking or riding an animal. They sail over the waters by means of mechanically driven ships. They have soared into the air with the birds. They have even reached the moon. Thus a study of geography is all-embracing. We may start with an investigation of some local feature, but we soon find ourselves involved in endless other matters that are interdependent.

Yet in many schools, geography has been relegated to a minor place. It has even been abolished as a subject in itself and included in Social Studies. Perhaps the reason for this is that the purpose of teaching this particular subject has been overlooked, together with the more fundamental aspects of education, in favour of examinations. Another point may well be that programmed learning is in fashion but geography does not lend itself well to this type of instruction.

One good reason why geography should have its rightful place in the school curriculum is that we no longer live in isolated communities. Our world is shrinking. For the peasant of past centuries, toiling on his land, what happened in the next village was perhaps of little consequence. Today, we have a world economy. We have world communications. We have world problems. People travel as never before. These are factors that make the teaching of geography as a school subject more important than ever before.

Another reason for proper geography teaching is the effect it has on the growing mind. The comprehensive nature of the subject gives it a special quality of *wholeness*. It belongs to both sciences and humanities. It deals with many different things, yet each of these is a part of a whole. It also has a very human aspect. It tells how human beings live and work, whatever their occupation or country.

In addition to what is purely informative and the consideration of the effect of imparting information, we must make allowance for the fact that we are dealing with varying age groups. The first task is to clarify our minds as to the aims of education. Secondly, we need to know something of child development; then thirdly, we can discuss details of material and method.

In the author's book *Commonsense Schooling,* an attempt was made to define the purposes of education. These are listed as:

—training in intellectual and manipulative skills;
—an awakening of social conscience;
—cultivation of means of self-expression;
—spiritual development.

Geography is a subject par excellence for these matters. It may not be rated high in the stakes for university entrance, but for general cultural education, it has no equal.

With regard to the training of skills, a high intellectual ability must be developed to understand the complexities of geographical relationships. Conversely, the attempt to understand and the exercise in grasping these relationships will further intellectual development. Accurate observation and reporting are necessary; so is logical thinking. What might be termed a "geographical imagination" must be developed; that is to say: the ability to appreciate landscapes, situations and living conditions vicariously. Manipulative skill is required for modelling and mapmaking.

Of all subjects, geography perhaps lends itself best to awakening a feeling of social responsibility. By social responsibility, we mean the awareness of, and consideration for, other people and other modes of life. The earth is the living space and the workplace of all human beings, whether black or white, yellow or brown. All humanity shares the earth, the air, the water, the influences from outer space. It must be possible in the teaching of geography to give a real feeling that peoples and countries other than our own actually do exist and that different colors on a map are only symbols for something very definite. Wide knowledge is the best antidote for narrow-mindedness. Chauvinism or parochialism is not to be combatted by directives to be more liberal, but liberalism is an attitude of mind achieved indirectly through many-sided studies. To know is to understand. International goodwill is better fostered by an objective study of foreign countries than by superficial get-togethers. Foreigners have different viewpoints from ours. A German history of the Great War reads quite differently from an English one. On the field of Agincourt there is a rather dilapidated monument in memory of the French who died there. One immediately gets a different impression of this famous battle. Certainly the views of the Native Americans and the European immigrants on the settlement of America would hardly coincide. Ethics and standards vary in different parts of the world. A knowledge of these matters cannot help but broaden the mind.

Since we have a world economy, the use of the world's resources is everybody's business. Is it a pleasant thought that one in every three of the world's population is undernourished? There are diseases that are the concern of every nation. The whole question of pollution is now very much in the public mind. Water is polluted, so is the atmosphere. Natural resources are limited. Humanity has a responsibility to the earth itself, if only in self-interest. Geography shows the interdependence of the human being and nature, and also demonstrates the necessity for wide cooperation.

In the matter of self-expression, there are accounts and descriptions to be written, pictorial and other maps to be made, also sketches, drawings, paintings, models.

When we speak of spiritual development here, we are not referring to metaphysics, but to the stretching of the mind through material contacts. Human beings live in space. They need an orientation in space to feel at home in their surroundings. A huge amount of material and interesting knowledge has to be garnered and coordinated into a comprehensive world-picture. There is joy to the spirit in discovery, spiritual activity in enlivening the imagination. A feeling of satisfaction and consolidation is produced with the realization that earth is "home." Although it sounds paradoxical, we could say that geography gives a child a spiritual experience by putting him "on his feet."

Because there are so many different aspects of geography, it is difficult to set up a syllabus. In mathematics one can start with simple sums and concepts and proceed to more difficult ones. This is not the case with geography, where there are no particularly easy or especially difficult parts. A further problem is that its comprehensive nature demands that one go a little beyond obvious material manifestations. The earth has its rhythms; it has its breathing in and breathing out. It has a sort of life-process. Different forces radiate from it in different parts of the globe, and these affect the racial and geographical varieties of human beings. The world must be seen as a whole.

It is the chronological age of the child and the parallel mental development that give a clue as to what to teach, when, and how. A syllabus that states: first year (age eleven) British Isles; second, Europe; third, the Americas; fourth, Australia; etc., pays no regard to the fact that children learn differently at different ages, that their educational needs vary, and that as a natural sequence, both matter and approach must be different at different ages.

Children have an expanding consciousness. They are reaching out for new knowledge and experiences. At the same time as they make an attempt to digest these, they further their development. The path is from story, through factual description, to perception and judgement.

Let us also remind ourselves of two golden rules that apply to general teaching as well as to geography. The first is that what children learn to love in the early years, they will understand later. Thus, early teaching must be imaginative and appeal to the feelings. The second rule is that the teacher must teach with enthusiasm. This has the effect of stimulating the life forces.

Let us also be aware of the desirability of cultivating a sense of reverence, of curiosity, and wonder in children. These lay a foundation for morality.

Summarising our observations on the nature of the child, let us remember that from the age of six to nine the child is still living partly in his or her own dream world. From nine to twelve some interest develops in the outer world, but still the mind requires pictures rather than explanations. From twelve to fourteen, physical maturity brings with it greater interest in the physical world and a growing desire to understand connections. During all these years (six to fourteen) the child's nature demands a pictorial-descriptive approach, tending towards the rational-conceptual from twelve onwards. After fourteen, the mind opens out in all directions and demands explanations, cohesion, and knowledge of cause and effect. The nature of the adolescent is often thoughtful and introspective, and in geography, as in every other subject, this is something to be dealt with educationally.

In a general way, the material given to children up to the age of twelve will be a description of the gifts of the earth. This fosters a feeling of responsibility if it can be indicated in some way that a gift has to be used, or that it calls forth some reciprocal action. From twelve to fourteen, the general trend will be to describe the uses of the gifts of earth by human beings. From fourteen onwards the study will be of the how and why of all matters, such as, for instance, the structure of the earth, the economy, communications, culture.

Up to the age of nine, there will be no geography instruction as such. That is not the same as saying that geography should not be taught. Indeed, this is the vital age for laying the foundations. It is possible at this age to introduce many aspects of geography—or perhaps better said—it is not necessary to introduce them, it is only necessary to call attention to phenomena. What child has not tried to build a seawall of sand, only to have it washed away by the tides. After a rainstorm he or she will notice how little rivulets are made in a soft path. Those fortunate to live in Derbyshire in England, or the neighbouring counties may know Mam Tor, with the impressive nickname, The Shivering Mountain. This is because the surface of one face is continuously sliding earthwards. In the same district are limestone caves hollowed out by the action of streams. In Yorkshire and Dartmoor are isolated standing stones of peculiar shapes caused by the eroding action of the winds. A child may be interested to look at the soft clay cliffs of part of the Yorkshire coast where houses may be seen toppling into the sea and learn that out to sea are drowned Anglo-Saxon villages. In Harlech the sea used to come right up to the castle, and this is the way supplies were brought. Now the sea is two miles away. The things that interest a child are endless, but for this age the teacher should be careful not to enter too deeply into scientific explanations. The coastal erosion and the receding sea are battles between the elements. Now the water gains victory and now earth.

A brook, with its swirling waters, curved course, overhanging banks and round pebbles, can provide many a geography lesson. This can be supported on, or even built around, a poem such as "The Brook," by Tennyson.

> I come from haunts of coot and hern,
> I make a sudden sally,
> And sparkle out among the fern,
> To bicker down a valley. . . .

Note that the brook is animate and this is how young children appreciate things. For them all creation is alive and their minds are best stimulated when the sun, moon, wind, flowers and animals engage in lively conversation with one another. There are many poems dealing with the seasons, weather, winds, the sea and the hills which can provide the necessary inspiration.

In dealing with a theme such as this, one should be careful not to destroy the language. The best approach is for the teacher to digest the material first, talk about it, explain where necessary and then give the poem at the end as a sort of culmination. The language should be left to speak for itself, and nothing further of an analytical nature should be undertaken.

In England we must give, for the most part, an imaginative picture of what a mountain is. There is a wonderful description in George MacDonald's story of "The Princess and Curdie." It is too long to quote in full, but here are a few excerpts:

> They (the mountains) are portions of the heart of the earth that have escaped from the dungeon down below and rushed up and out. For the heart of the earth is a great wallowing mass, not of blood, as in the hearts of men and animals, but of glowing hot melted metals and stones. Out of that cauldron certain bubbles have bubbled out and escaped —up and away, and there they stand in the cool, cold sky—mountains . . . . Think of the creatures scampering over and burrowing in it and the birds building their nests upon it, and the trees growing out of its sides, like hair to clothe it, and the lovely grass in the valleys. And along with all these, think of the terrible precipices down which the traveller may fall and be lost, and the frightful gulfs of blue air trapped in the glaciers. But the inside, who shall tell what lies there? Caverns of awfullest solitude, their walls miles thick, sparkling with ores of gold or silver, perhaps a brook, cold and babbling. . . .

All these things then are physical geography, yet not by name. Nor should they be approached scientifically or too factually. For children of this age, let us always bear in mind that there is a living quality even in inanimate nature. Let them observe, let the teacher point out, but then let the matter be clothed in story form, without explanations. The above is a description belonging to a story. An example of a geographical story pure and simple would be something like this:

The Playground of the Winds

On a wide moorland, high up on the hills, in a place open to sun and sky, with no forests or trees nearby, there once stood some great rocks. It was a place where the winds liked to play. In the spring lively little breezes blew over the frost and snow; in the summer, a gentle wind from the sea; but in the autumn great gales blew across it and in winter came the north wind full of snow and ice. The winds whistled around these great huge rocks, sometimes trying to blow them over, but the rocks stood firm and told them to do their worst, they could not be moved. So the winds blew and the rocks stood firm and the winds blew and the rocks still stood firm. The winds began to feel sorry for those old great rocks standing up there so lonely. They said, "We travel all over the land and see many, many things, and we have a wonderful life, but you stand there, and stand there and stand there. You see nothing and nobody sees you. You look cold and gaunt and lonely. Let us improve your looks. We know how to do sculpture and we can help you." At first the rocks were not too pleased and just wanted to be left alone but finally they thought it might be nice to have some company besides their own so they agreed. The winds set to work. The south wind blew, then the east, then the north and then the west. They all did some work but it was the south and the west winds who worked the hardest. They worked hard and long, blowing away a little bit off one rock here and another bit off another rock there, until, instead of those great big plump shapes, the rocks began to take on different forms. One day some people happened to take a walk that way and a man suddenly stopped and said, "Good gracious, look at that rock; it looks like a frog." So they called it the Frog Rock. When the winds heard this, they worked harder still and gradually all those old stones got turned into something which could have a name: The Oyster Shell, Indian's Head, Sleeping Hare, Mushroom Rock, Donald Duck, Cow's Head, the Elephant, the Owl, and many more, and (to the children) if you ever go to a place called Brimham in Yorkshire, you will see these things and many others for yourselves.

Observations can naturally be made on the weather. The children will notice whether it is hot or cold, raining or sunny and suitable stories can be told. The observations can be supported again by poems such as the following by Cecily E. Pike, in which we have a characterisation of a living being:

> Look out, look out,
> Jack Frost is about.
> He's after our fingers and toes;
> And, all through the night,
> The gay little sprite
> Is working where nobody knows.

The rain cycle can be put into story form:

> Once upon a time there was a cloud floating from the sea toward the land and as she looked down she saw that the fields looked brown, the leaves on the trees were hanging limp; people were looking anxiously at their wells and reservoirs of water and she realised that everything down there was very dry. So she steered towards the mountains on the land and said to her children, the raindrops who were clustered around her, "I want you to go to earth for a while. Jump when I get near the mountains." So the raindrops left their home in the sky and splattered down to earth, bringing refreshment to the flowers and plants and trees, animals and humans, who were all very thankful. Then slowly the raindrops made their way into the springs and brooks and rivers and flowed out again to the sea. It was tremendous fun to join the waves and get mixed up with the great ocean. Sometimes they looked at the sky, thinking of the earlier journey they had made and when the sun sent some strong beams down to the water, some of the raindrops crawled up the sunbeams into the sky again. There they made themselves another home which the human beings call a cloud. Soon they were sailing through the sky again, and who knows, perhaps that is the very cloud which we can see above us.

A poem to support this is Shelley's "The Cloud," surely one of the most beautiful poems in the English language:

I bring fresh showers for the thirsting flowers,
From the seas and the streams;
I bear light shade for the leaves when laid
In their noonday dreams.
From my wings are shaken the dews that waken
The sweet buds everyone,
When rocked to rest on their mother's breast,
As she dances about the sun.
I wield the flail of the lashing hail,
And whiten the green plains under,
And then again, I dissolve it in rain,
And laugh as I pass in thunder.

Perhaps one verse, as above, is sufficient and it is no great matter whether the whole thing is understood in detail. The language, the rhythm, the melody are sufficient. A further theme would concern itself with plants or flowers found in the district.

> A little gnome once found a big brown seed which he thought needed to be cared for. So he found a nice patch of ground belonging to some people who loved the little folk and he carefully buried it. The rain fairies sent rain, and the warmth fairies sent warmth and soon one little shoot came out of the seed and went downwards into the earth and another went upwards above the ground where the air fairies could dance around it. The stalk grew upwards and leaves came out but still it grew until it was bigger than a man. At last a beautiful big flower came out at the top of the stalk with a big round shining face like the sun itself. So people called it the Sunflower.

Here we have a living introduction to the elements of earth, water, fire, and air. In this connection the author has made good use of the choruses of the elementals from his play entitled "The Golden Key" contained in the booklet *Miscellany*. They are, however, too long to quote here. A shorter poem by Rosemary Gebert, useful in this respect, is:

Busy gnomes
Bring to birth
Little seeds
In the earth.

Watersprites
Feed the shoots
Striving upwards
From the roots.

Airy sylphs
Power bestow,
Help the plant
To thrive and grow.

Sunsprites bring
Warming gold.
Rainbow hued
Buds unfold.

Flowers all
Secrets keep.
In their hearts
New seeds sleep.

Water, fire,
Earth and air,
In their growth
Have a share,
That a seed
A seed may bear.

An archetypal story which illustrates the connection between soil and natural vegetation is that of the legend of the heather on the mountain, found in the children's storybook *The Key of the Kingdom*. This tells the story of the mountain that wanted companionship but no plant could live there except the heather.

Animal stories (if one can reckon these as geography) exist in abundance or they are not difficult to make up. The food we eat and the clothes we wear also provide themes. The teacher is reminded that no scientific explanations are required at this age and certainly no utilitarian aspects such as a giraffe having a long neck to feed from the tops of the trees. Simple, imaginative stories or descriptions are all that are required.

It may be possible to visit a farm where the wealth of material is endless. A visit to the seaside of specially interesting localities will be geographically useful. Perhaps there are some factories near so that manufacturing industries can be included in an elementary way, possibly coal mines. There will certainly be a bus route or a railway line not far away, and lucky or unlucky, according to viewpoint, some air transport overhead.

At the age of eight or nine, children often become collectors, perhaps of seashells or crystals, and these again can lead to conversations, stories, descriptions, which are all, in some form, geographical knowledge. There is a delightful story of St. Hilda, quoted here as a good example of a suitable presentation.

> When St. Hilda took charge of the monastery at Whitby, the district round about was inhabited by snakes. She prayed that they might be thrown into the sea, and then with her whip, drove these poisonous snakes to the edge of the cliff, where they tumbled into the sea coiled up like watch springs. When they hit the rocks below, they were turned into stone. Some can still be found. Today people call them Ammonites.

There are various King Arthur legends which belong to different parts of the country. In Glastonbury Abbey is the Glastonbury Thorn, reputed to be descended from the staff of Joseph of Arimathea, who landed near this spot with the cup used at the Last Supper. The cup itself is supposedly buried under a local spring. But other parts of the country also have their share of useful stories.

The lake into which Sir Bedivere threw the sword Excalibur is supposedly in South Wales. Tennyson describes it truly:

> On one side lay the ocean,
> And on one, lay a great water,
> And the moon was full.

The writer has only experienced this place by daylight, but even so it seemed to possess a magic charm. Such legends bring life to the teaching.

A good theme for the nine- or ten-year-old children would be to study the course of a river. One would describe how the springs bubble out of the hillside. Attention would be drawn to the flora and fauna of the immediate surroundings. As the stream gathers strength, it rushes down the hillside through rocky clefts and possibly flows through woods, which can also be described in detail. It then comes into the plain, broadening out and slowing its flow and it becomes closely connected with human occupations. Finally it reaches the sea and merges with the ocean. If it is done tactfully, a parallel can be drawn with human life and the geography becomes almost a religion lesson.

In a main lesson period for this age is a study entitled Practical Activities. Its purpose is to introduce children to practical life since they are now at the age when interest in the physical world develops. But one of the practical subjects is Farming and Gardening, which obviously has geographical connections and should be considered in arranging any other work.

With the age of ten, the children are ready for a more conscious look at their immediate surroundings. The theme at this age should be the story of the town, village or district where they live, which is actually dealt with in the main lesson period known as Home Surroundings. It should be coordinated with any geographical teaching given otherwise.

The subject is still not exactly geography but it is an account of the historical and geographical features of the neighbourhood, also of the flora and fauna. Naturally, topics such as occupations, connections between natural resources and human living conditions, and communications are considered. Geographical terms and concepts should be introduced in these early lessons and the children will then be familiar with them when dealing with other parts of the earth. They will enjoy the terminology.

The modern cliche of "let the children find out" does not wear particularly well in practice. There is too much to find out. Even the teacher has to do considerable research for such work. Let the children add to the sum total by their own discoveries by all means but in the main it is the teacher who does the teaching. Of course the children must participate, not only by listening. They can retell what has been explained, orally or in writing, or both. They can draw, model, or paint objects, an activity which is a sort of digestive process. They can, with or without guidance, observe the environment and draw a map, making it perhaps pictorial instead of symbolic, i.e., they draw a little train on the railway track instead of just a line; they put a cow in a field instead of just shading. Where there is a conifer forest, they sketch a few fir trees.

Participation also includes visits to local spots of special interest. Folk tales or legends connected with any particular local feature (St. Hilda, above) will also add impressiveness to the subject.

Since examples will convey the idea much better than explanations, an outline is given here of material relating to two different types of places—Leeds in the industrial north and Edenbridge, a small town in the Weald of Kent—based on the author's own experience. Sketches, maps, local folklore, etc., must be added.

Perhaps the best approach is to ask the children about the place concerned. They will have quite a lot to say and the conversation might lead, say in the case of Leeds, to the names of certain streets right in the middle of the city: Boar Lane, Swinegate, Mill Hill. How does it come that names of such obvious country origin are used in what is now the busiest part of the city? Having elicited a great deal of information, the story could begin. Obviously, what is given here is spread over a period of time.

THE STORY OF LEEDS

Leeds is called the city of a thousand trades. It is a busy city. There is a lot of traffic and many people move about in the city. Underground are miles of pipes to provide gas, electricity, water and to take waste away. There are lots of factories and works, such as brickworks, engineering shops, tanneries, foundries. Then there are factories for making crisps and cream crackers. But above all, Leeds is famous for its clothing industries. We shall learn how it grew to be so important for clothing as well as for steel manufacture and other things.

The city lies between hills and plain. A valley runs through it in which flows the river Aire.

There was a time when this district looked very different from the way it appears now. It consisted of forests and swamps. The Kelts were the first people who lived here and a tribe called the Brigantes lived in this area. The Druids were their priests and we can find some Druid circles in the neighbourhood. The names of the rivers and mountains are Keltic, as, for instance, the rivers Aire and Wharfe, the hill known as Chevin, and the mountain Pen-y-ghent.

The Romans came to Britain, then the Anglo-Saxons, followed by the Vikings, and finally the Normans. We know where the different peoples had settlements because of the place names. Those ending in *-ley, -ton, -ham,* and *-ing* were Anglo-Saxon. The names of Viking settlements end in *-thorpe, -wick,* and *-by*.

Leeds was first mentioned in Anglo-Saxon times, and its name probably comes from Loidis, a Keltic chieftan. Headingley, which is now a part of Leeds, was a clearing in the forest belonging to the family of Haedda. In Anglo-Saxon times, monks came from Iona and the north to preach Christianity, and we find their names attached to churches in the city.

The Normans made a survey of England, and Leeds is mentioned. It tells us that thirty-five small farmers lived there and they owned fourteen ploughs. There was a church, a priest, a mill and ten acres of meadow. We know, therefore, that at that time Leeds was a small farming village on the north bank of the River Aire at a point where it could be crossed. It is believed that the Romans had earlier had a ford there.

A monastery was built in the Aire valley as in many other Yorkshire vales, and this one, Kirkstall, now a ruin, is in one of the city parks. The monks worked in iron which they found, and there has been a foundry nearby ever since.

For a long time there was not much change but eventually Leeds grew to be a little market town. The reason for this was that sheep were raised in the hills and in those days cloth was also spun at home. The village was a convenient place for buyers and sellers of wool and cloth to meet. English cloth was sold abroad even in those days but transport was not so easily arranged. From Leeds the goods could be taken down to the river.

Then came the time when machines were invented, and as it happened, on the doorstep of Leeds were coal, clay, iron, and sand—all the necessary things for making machinery. So the village grew to a town and the town grew to a city, with all its present industries, houses, transport, utilities, etc.

The above, of course, is only an indication. Many of the themes can be developed ad lib. Here is another example:

Many years ago, most of England was covered with forests. There were thick forests of oak trees where Edenbridge and the surrounding villages now stand. Wandering tribes of people lived here called the Kelts.

Just before the birth of Christ, the Romans visited Britain and later settled there. They fought the Kelts and gradually drove them westwards and northwards into the countries now known as Wales and Scotland, where one can still hear the old Keltish language spoken.

The Romans called one of the first tribes they met the Cantii and this is where the name Kent comes from. The Romans built many straight roads in Britain. One went through what is now known as Edenbridge on its way from London to Lewes. In those days the latter was a port.

After the Romans had left Britain, the Jutes and Anglo-Saxons came from what is now Germany. They began to clear spaces in the forests in order to grow crops. The Saxons had a settlement near the present River Eden where the Roman road had crossed it. They built or rebuilt a bridge which was named after one of their chieftains, Eadelme. Thus this place became known as Eadelme'sbrege, which has become shortened to Edenbridge. The Saxons also built a church, but that has disappeared and another one has been built on the same site.

In the following centuries the Vikings or Norsemen visited England, mainly for the purpose of plundering.

In 1066 the Normans conquered England and the name Eadelme'sbrege is found mentioned in one of their documents of 1114. The Normans became the masters and the Saxons the servants. About 1236 a manor house for the Norman Lord of the Manor was built. Nowadays a new housing estate occupies the area, but the name has remained—Manor House Estate. As far as the use of the land was concerned, nothing much changed. The Saxons had made clearings in the forest and the people continued to grow their crops and keep cattle, sheep and pigs.

A mill was built by the river in 1300 and this was still in use in 1967, although then driven by electricity and not by water. Rich people from the city who liked to have a country house came into the district. One reason was that the road from London runs for the most part on the downs [ME *doun* 'hill': generally treeless uplands with thin soil], and that meant a road which was always passable, whereas roads on the clay were often mudtracks. One family which came to Edenbridge was called Stangrove, and the name still lingers in Stangrove Park. Another was Delaware, and there is still a Delaware farm. The Lord Mayor of London built himself a house in Edenbridge. This is the Taylour House, which is still there, although now it is an antique shop. A coach house was built in 1465 to accommodate travellers, and this is also still there. It is the Crown.

In 1673 a tanyard was opened; now the area is a shopping precinct. Then there was a flourishing shoemaking business. There must have been a lot of grain grown in the district, because in 1812 another mill was built, but this time a windmill. The sails have gone, but the stump is still to be seen. There were a lot of trees, because we know that at this time there was also a timber trade. During these years there were toll gates at both ends of the village—one on the road to Crockham Hill and the other at Den Cross. The toll gates have now disappeared.

About a hundred years ago, Edenbridge was linked up with other towns and cities by railways. Now, with the coming of cars and buses, the roads have been resurfaced and there is more road traffic than rail. London County Council has housed some of its people here on new estates and a factory area has been provided so that work is available locally. Edenbridge still remains, however, a district of fields, farms, trees, and fresh air.

Now would be the time to introduce map work. One can explain how things look from different viewpoints, e.g., how we should see things if we were hovering in a helicopter. Thus we can start marking roads, railways, prominent buildings, etc. on a map.

Children can then find out and list or write about other features of the district, e.g., the wildflowers, native trees, farm crops, factories. They can name the banks and the pubs, classify the shops, describe the location and/or appearance of the post office, the railway station, the church, fire station, etc.

Having introduced a fair number of geographical ideas, and with the child's consciousness expanding, the description of the immediate surroundings should be extended downwards. In general, the idea is to take an area within a limited radius of the home town or village and, if possible, it should be something that can be dealt with as a unit. As far as the teaching in Great Britain is concerned, this could mean the whole of the country. It can be done in stages. For example, perhaps from Leeds one would first deal with the whole of Yorkshire; from Edenbridge, the Weald. The chief emphasis should be on descriptions, supported by the children's own observations and knowledge.

The natural resources (the gifts of earth and nature) should be described together with the way they influence living conditions. The human element must always be brought into the picture. At this stage it is not necessary to take things in any particular sequence.

According to taste, need, or interest of the children, the teacher could take regional studies, i.e., the interpretation of phenomena that give character to a particular region—or take a single phenomenon and explain its distribution and significance over the whole of an area (systematic studies). Matters might be mixed. Examples of regional studies in the British Isles would be:

—the Potteries
the Fens
—the Thames Valley
—the Industrial West Riding
—a single city or county
—London certainly merits a special study.

As an introduction, it might be quite good to make an imaginary journey. Suppose one starts at Dover, traverses the gardens of Kent, crosses London for the moment, and comes into the rich farming country to the north of the capital. Some deviation to the east brings one to the Fens, while excursions west would mean visiting various industrial cities. Travelling north one might see the cathedrals of Lincoln and York, the farming country of the Vale of York, and not far away the industrial West Riding. According to taste, one travels to Newcastle or Edinburgh or then into Scotland, and returns via the Lake District, Manchester, and its satellites, Cheshire, a possible deviation into Wales, back to Birmingham, Vale of Evesham, Gloucester, Bristol, Devon, Cornwall, and back somewhere through the southern counties. So one gives a sort of bird''s eye view. Systematic studies would be:

—sheep farming
—shipbuilding
—coal mining
—crop or dairy farming
—ports
—communications

Gradually the single pictures will merge together into a cohesive whole, naturally supported by map work. Although pictorial maps will probably appeal most to the children in their own creative activity, they can also begin to study Ordnance Survey maps or others with representative symbols.

The pattern of work for twelve year olds is similar but extending into further regions of the earth. It would seem natural in England to proceed to make some studies of Europe next, but since England has very intimate connections (language, race) with more distant parts of the earth, there is no reason why this path could not be followed if it is preferred.

Again, this could be regional—a coherent picture of a specific place, or systematic—one phenomenon over a wide area, e.g. deserts, forests, on a world scale. Eventually one has to deal with each country in any case, giving a picture of all aspects—relief, climate, natural resources, agriculture, industry, characteristics and nature of the people, not forgetting the introduction of support material such as manners, dress, language, music. In order to savour the *wholeness* of a country, Dr. Steiner suggests that in the case of Japan, for example, children should be encouraged to paint in the Japanese style.

Quite simple things are often very illustrative. For example, if one has sufficient knowledge of German, one might not only produce examples of the way the language sounds but also the complicated and apparently sometimes unending sentence structure. American English, Cockney, Australian, and their equivalents relative to other parts of the world might be demonstrated.

Examples might be brought of Chinese or Indian music. One of the author's favorite stories is of sitting by the water's edge in Hawaii on Christmas Eve, dripping with perspiration and listening to the hula girls playing "Silent Night" on the Hawaiian guitar.

Dress and costumes can be shown in pictures or photographs, and customs form an endless source of inspiration. For example: driving on the left or right, nose-rubbing, the habit of some Europeans of shaking hands on every possible occasion, praying habits of the Mohammedans.

There is, however, at twelve, a special element which must be taken into consideration in relation to human development. This is one of the priorities before mentioned.

We said that at twelve a greater interest develops in the material world. But it is not only a question of greater interest. For its development, the child's mind needs to come into closer contact with matter. It is, therefore, the logical thing at this age to introduce some form of geology. The actual study should perhaps better be termed lithology, the science of the nature and composition of stones and rocks.

Attention should be called to the tremendous changes which have taken place on the earth during countless years. The ice sheets once covered parts of Europe and when these melted, valleys were scraped out. The crust of the earth has folded, making the strata bend. Sea fossils are found on mountain tops, and the remains of forests under the sea. Rivers change their courses, new land is formed by deltas.

There are three types of rock to be described: sedimentary, igneous, and metamorphic, with examples in each classification. It is of particular interest to study a piece of limestone where one finds the fossils readily and to realize that this rock (like chalk) is formed of organic material, of once living creatures.

There is also the connection between geology and landscape. Some mention should be made of metals and precious stones.

In connection with geological studies, the students can draw river systems and different mountain shapes, showing how these are influenced by the different types of rock.

Thus the ages of ten, eleven, twelve, are the time to learn about many aspects of the earth, including rock formations, from descriptions. But from now onwards (and this is a priority) it is necessary to take a fresh look at the world as the demand arises in the student's mind to know how and why.

At the age of thirteen, with the widening horizon of the mind, students should be learning in history about the Age of Discovery, the great explorations; this study links with and obviously supports the studies of geography. At this age, students read by themselves and therefore much background and support material can be given for individual study. The biographies of the great explorers are particularly valuable since the student can also appreciate the strength of these intrepid personalities who may very well inspire emulation. In this connection we think of Henry the Navigator, Vasco da Gama, Diaz, Columbus, Magellan, Cabot, Francis Drake. Traveller's tales or stories based in a particular setting can also add knowledge, for example, those of Gerald Durell. Personal experiences are, of course, invaluable.

Any time from now on is right for an introduction to mathematical geography, i.e., those matters which need a conceptual thinking rather than an imaginative one. One poses the questions: Why do we have day and night? Why do we have seasons? If it is now ten o'clock in England, is it ten o'clock elsewhere in the world? Thus we come to deal with the course of the sun and the moon, earth gyrations, and to such matters as latitude and longitude, equator, tropics of Cancer and Capricorn, arctic and antarctic circles. One can take a step into astronomy and include some knowledge of the constellations and movements of the planets.

This is the age too, for learning all sorts of things about culture in connection with geography. One could compare for instance, the life of an Eskimo [Inuit] with that of a South Sea Islander. In the former case, nature decrees a hard and never-ending struggle for existence. By contrast, the Tongan islander plants his two hundred banana trees on attaining his majority and can go on fishing or sitting in the sun or doing whatever takes his fancy. One might say something about the extraordinary supersensory powers of Australian aboriginals. One might compare a densely populated country like Japan with a sparsely populated one like Norway. Chinese and American culture make a good contrast. One might even put such a question as to what life in Britain would be like were it not an island.

Thus by the end of the thirteenth year, a general picture of the whole world should be completed. The student should know something about the earth's structure, climate, vegetation, animals, natural resources, industries, communications, peoples, as well as having a picture in mind of all these things in relation to a particular country. This may sound overambitious. It is therefore worth repeating that teaching has to be *symptomatic*. If necessary, it should be possible to give an impression of, say, Australia, in one or two lessons. Details of population, gross national income, car production and such matters are of no consequence at this stage.

The main stress will have been on economics (in the general sense of production and distribution), culture (way of living), with some idea of political divisions (countries and states). All studies will have been centred on the human being and the relationship between human being and environment—anthrogeography. With the growth of the reasoning faculty and the demand to know how and why comes the understanding for cause and effect. With the growth of physical maturity comes a different attitude to, and understanding of, the physical world. So, in a certain sense, geography begins again. We have built up a world picture from single items; now we look at the world as a whole and see how the single bits fit, with special regard to reasons.

Some of the things given in story form earlier can now be explained scientifically. Earlier we told such stories as "The Cloud," "The Heather on the Mountain," and "The Playground of the Winds." It is a wonderful experience to stand in front of a class and say, "Do you remember the story I told you a long time ago about . . ." and then to explain the facts. "I once told you about some rocks at Brimham in Yorkshire, with peculiar shapes and names." Now an explanation somewhat as follows could be given:

> These rocks appear on the skyline like huge ruins and they are about 950 feet above sea level. Each rock is a huge mass and could weigh up to 500 tons. At some time there was a violent upheaval in the earth's crust and these masses of millstone grit were thrust to the top. They were exposed to winds and sandstorms, heat, frost and moisture and so the softer parts got worn away, leaving these fantastic shapes.

It is from now on that reasons can be given concerning the movements in world trade and developments in industry—how civilizations are connected with economic conditions. There are also the historical connections and obviously the geography teaching must be coordinated with the physics, chemistry, and other lessons.

At fourteen, the students have a mental awareness sufficient to encompass the whole world. (In stating this we are assuming that up to now their education has been adequate). Their individual powers of perception and judgement are developing. At the same time there are other stirrings in the adolescent soul. While they are becoming more and more aware of the world in their expanding consciousness, they are also feeling their own individuality within, which brings a sense of loneliness and raises questions as to their own beings. They become thoughtful and introspective but at the same time need contact with people and wish to grapple with problems of the real world. They are now ready to question everything, including the evolution of the earth, the existence of God, the purpose of life. It is poor comfort to be told by the science teacher that the earth evolved accidentally from some gaseous matter, and from the religion teacher that God created the world. It is not very inspiring to learn that the earth is a cooling piece of dead matter revolving endlessly around the sun according to mechanical laws. It is even worse to be told that human existence is an accident and that possibly after life on earth there is nothing but the void.

It might be argued that it is not the task of the geography teacher to answer these questions and the student should be referred elsewhere, but education is a whole and if questions arise in this context, they had better be answered out of this context, as best we can. There must therefore be what might be termed a philosophical geography, or even a religious geography.

In showing cause and effect, we meet a need in the adolescent's soul. We can show that relief is the result of erosion, that the volume of water in a river is due to geology, weather and topography, that vegetation depends on climate. The realization will dawn that there is a pattern in existence and we may be emboldened to say that as nothing happens "by accident," why should we not assume some prime cause in the making and sustaining of the world? We do not want to dogmatize, but we can sow seeds. In other lessons, the stories of other civilizations and the changing outlook of their peoples may also point in the same direction.

This is an undertone. The study of geography itself, with its tremendous scope and wide interests, is in itself a panacea.

At the age of fourteen, then, the students should look at the world again from their newly acquired world-consciousness, this time in its entirety. They should learn to appreciate the earth as a whole organism, for the maintenance of which they have responsibility. To this end they must understand human dependence on the products of the earth, mineral and vegetable—how human intervention can affect climate, fertility and population. They must learn about economic aspects of natural resources.

One theme is that the earth is a unit shared by all who live on it, irrespective of colour, race, and beliefs. People have built empires in the attempt to dominate the world, but they have crumbled. Now economy is worldwide, and all sorts of examples can be brought here to show, for instance, how raw materials are found in one place, transported to another, formed into something else and the finished product sent elsewhere. A good example would be to take the production of a newspaper—and it is not only a question of the paper but the ink, the machinery, and even the contributors and contents.

A further suggestion would be to take some commodity, as, for example, timber and gather all information together concerning origin, growth and eventual use—or one could take a region or a particular country and show how it fits in with the pattern of the rest of the world.

Another theme would be industry, or transport and communications in their worldwide ramifications. It is not so long ago that most people had little or no contact with the rest of the world. Now world communications are in some respects instantaneous. The crossing of the oceans was at one time an arduous task. Now it can be a matter of a few hours. Transport, of course, has to do with the distribution of goods, and students should get a picture of the main streams of transport.

Parallel with this and bearing in mind the adolescent's growing preoccupation with the material world, with cause and effect, a further theme would concern itself with a more detailed study of geology. One could look at the mountain ranges in Europe and trace the four foldings, now separated by water or new soils. The most ancient range of mountains in Europe has its remains in the outer Hebrides and the Lofoten Islands off the coast of Norway. The rock of these islands is the oldest known and belongs to the Azoic age. Azoic means 'without life', and these rocks contain no traces of living organisms.

The second range consists of the mountains of northern Ireland, Scotland, northern England and Scandinavia. These too are ancient rocks but show no traces of life. They belong to the Paleozoic age.

The third folding is more recent and more widely spread. The mountains belong to the Mezozoic age in which we find the first traces of animal existence. They consist of much softer rock and have therefore been much weathered down. They appear as hill and plateau in southern Ireland, southwest England, France, Germany, Spain, Bohemia, and parts of Eastern Europe.

The most recent of the four foldings produced the Alps and their extensions into northern Spain and North Africa westwards, and eastwards to the Caucasus, mountains of Asia Minor, and beyond. There is therefore a tremendous belt of mountains stretching across Europe in an east-west direction.

From the study of the mountain formations in Europe and Asia, one could look at the mountains of the Americas, which by contrast have a north-south direction. It would appear that some different formative force has been at work.

Further studies in geology can be made continuing the work already started—volcanoes, earthquakes, erosion, and a more detailed study of the geology of the immediate neighbourhood would be in place here.

Although the above accords with the age of the student and meets a particular need, it is not necessarily exclusive and other geographical studies can be pursued as opportunity permits.

Continuing the work of the previous class and having looked at the mountain formations on a world scale, it would now be opportune, for **students aged fifteen**, to make a special study of the Alps.

The structure should be described, i.e., folds of limestone and granite. The Alps are the source of two of Europe's great rivers, the Rhine and the Rhone, while the Danube skirts its northern boundaries. A great deal of what is called physical geography can be studied in connection with these mountains and one learns these things then as realities and not as abstractions. Physical geography has to do with the formation of valleys, types of valleys, sources of springs, peneplains, etc.

One should extend the picture by describing how many sources of life and culture meet in the Alps. There has been a meeting of the peoples here. Switzerland, one of the smallest countries in Europe, has four national languages: German, French, Italian, and Romansch. Austria has long been a cultural centre.

The Alps are a natural dividing line in Europe. North of them is one type of vegetation and landscape; south, a totally different one with greater warmth and intense sunlight. In cultures the distinction can be seen, in peoples, in art.

The differences in cultures and outlooks could be extended to considerations on a world scale. Let us contrast the Chinese, for instance, with the Americans, in particular with the inhabitants of the U.S.A. On the one hand, an ancient civilization has continued for many hundreds of years without change until recent times. Its people's attitude to the world was one of philosophical acceptance. On the other hand, there is the hustling, bustling, world-transforming nature of the Americans. Does the configuration and nature of the land play a part in forming the human being? One could think of the mountains of America—the north-south direction—as following the lines of magnetic force, that is, a force intimately connected with the earth. Here is the most material civilization. In other respects one can also find contrasts, even in the stature of the human being. On average, the Chinese are short and sturdy, the Americans tall and slim, as were the original inhabitants of North America.

We have mentioned several times the expanding consciousness of the adolescent. As geology leads into the depths of the earth, now something more could be studied which leads to the heights—further studies in astronomy would be in place. There is an obvious necessity here for coordinating the work with the science teaching.

What happens between the earth and the heavens is also a study for this age, i.e., meteorology, the water cycle, cloud formation, cloud types, weather, factors influencing climate, climate and vegetation, ice ages, modern fears of global warming.

When the student is sixteen, physical geography is still the given theme, with the viewing of the earth as a physical whole. The following suggestions are given as indications:

One approach would be to draw some sort of comparison between the human being and the earth. One could speak of the four elements—earth, water, air, fire (warmth)—and relate these to the human being.

The human being has a threefold nature—head, rhythmic system, digestion. The earth also has a threefold nature. The quiet polar zone could be compared with the head, the temperate zone with the rhythmic system of heart and breathing, while the digestive system is like the torrid zone where everything is on the move.

It is interesting to note that a preponderance of the cultures that have had a major influence on world history have developed in the more-or-less temperate zone of the northern hemisphere: China, Japan, India, Persia, Babylon, Chaldea, Egypt, Greece, Israel, Palestine, Rome, Europe, Mexico. These countries all lie between 20 and 60 degrees north. Of course, there have also been significant contributions from cultures in the tropics: the three great kingdoms of Africa and the high cultures of South America.

There is a balance of land and sea on the earth; where there is a mass of land, we find a compensating mass of water. The poles are also balanced, sea at the north, land at the south. If one were to look imaginatively from the North Pole on all sides and the vision were sufficiently extended, one would see a broad line of land. From the South Pole one would only see the tips of continents.

The coast of Asia is broken by many islands; the coasts of America are straight, with the west coast descending abruptly from the mountains to the sea. In Europe and Africa there is a balance.

These are different ways then, of appreciating the shapes of the continents and possibly relating them to other factors. In connection with this, one could study such matters as Wegener's theory of continental drift. Other studies include: currents, winds, the earth's core. Some attention should be paid to flora and fauna generally in connection with geography, e.g., maize from America, is a solid, earthy grain; rice from the Far East, is a flowery, light type of grain, while the wheat of Europe is balanced between the two. The marsupials and their distribution would be another study.

Map drawing as a science is suitable for this class, e.g., Mercator projections. The work should be coordinated with surveying. Maps and the history of maps should be studied, i.e., mathematical geography, differing cultures and outlooks.

Assuming the students are still at school **at the age of seventeen and eighteen**, any general work is suitable. As a geographic-social study, a theme for this age would be the interrelationship of landscape, climate, vegetation and human activity in contrasting areas of the world. Another would be rocks and the associated scenery, also ecology.

World economy and its social impact should be considered—international trade and trade agreements with their results, genetically modified plants and animal cloning. Further studies can be made in depth in any field—regional, systematic or mathematical geography, paleontology, ethnography—but apart from specific lessons, pupils can work for themselves with tutorial guidance or through discussions, and try to assess world trends and world problems. The study almost becomes one of current affairs. One important theme would be to study the relationships between natural resources, capital and labour. Another might be to study the problem of pollution. Excellent suggestions are also to be found in a UNESCO book on geography:

- The political division of the earth's surface

- Economic life of the world
  - —currents of trade
  - —international trade

- Demographic problems
  - —growth of population
  - —overpopulation
  - —diseases, natural and social catastrophes

- Specifically geographic problems
  - —policies of changing the geographical and territorial development
  - —policies and problems of developing countries
  - —problems of the growth of towns

As a final study, students may well be invited to consider the three spheres of society: economics, politics, culture (spiritual life). Reference might be made to Rudolf Steiner's work in this field. Answers might be sought to the following questions:

- What is the relationship between economics and politics?
- How is spiritual life influenced by the other two?
- Would there not be a better distribution of resources if economic life were freed from politics?
- How far are politics influenced by economics?
- Should the spiritual life (i.e., church, education) not be entirely free to follow its own impulses without economic or political influence?
- In view of the impasse into which the present system has led us, is not some radical reorganization due?

Bibliography

The following are fundamental books by Rudolf Steiner on education.

Essentials of Education. Hudson, New York: Anthroposophic Press, 1997.

Discussions with Teachers. Hudson, New York: Anthroposophic Press, 1997.

The Foundations of Human Experience (also translated as *Study of Man*). Hudson, New York: Anthroposophic Press, 1996.

Human Values in Education. London: Rudolf Steiner Press, 1971.

The Kingdom of Childhood. Hudson, New York: Anthroposophic Press, 1995.

A Modern Art of Education. London: Rudolf Steiner Press, 1972.

Practical Advice to Teachers. London: Rudolf Steiner Press, 1976.

These titles are also available in editions published by Rudolf Steiner Press, 51, Queen Caroline Street, London, W6 9QL.

About the Author

Roy Wilkinson has been connected with the work of Rudolf Steiner for over 60 years. Born in Leicestershire, England, he was educated both locally and in Switzerland. He attended the Goetheanum School of Speech and Drama, receiving his certificate from Frau Dr. Steiner herself.

After working at an educational center, he made excursions into the fields of medicine (with Weleda) and agriculture, and eventually became a teacher. Over some forty years he taught in Steiner and state schools in England, Germany, and Switzerland. He has also taught children in need of special care.

Mr. Wilkinson has been active as an advisor to schools and lecturer on Rudolf Steiner education and Anthroposophy in many European countries, in South America as well as in English-speaking countries.

Another major contribution is the writing he has done over a period of more than twenty years. Wilkinson has produced introductory books on Rudolf Steiner education and its philosophical foundations. These and his curriculum guide booklets have been highly appreciated by teachers, parents, and those seeking answers to personal questions. A complete list of current editions is at the end of this volume.

BOOKS BY ROY WILKINSON

Questions and Answers on Rudolf Steiner Education
The Temperaments in Education
The Interpretation of Fairy Tales
The Curriculum of the Rudolf Steiner School
Commonsense Schooling
Rudolf Steiner on Education

Wilkinson Waldorf Curriculum Series:
Teaching English
Teaching Mathematics
Teaching Physics and Chemistry
Teaching Geography
Teaching History I: *Ancient Civilizations, Greece, Rome*
Teaching History II: *Middle Ages, Renaissance to the Second World War*
Old Testament Stories
Commentary on the Old Testament Stories
The Norse Stories and their Significance
Teaching Practical Activities: *Farming, Gardening, Housebuilding*
The Human Being and the Animal World
Plant Study and Geology
Nutrition, Health, and Anthropology
Miscellany: *A Collection of Poems and Plays*
Plays for Puppets

The Origin and Development of Language
The Spiritual Basis of Rudolf Steiner Education

Rudolf Steiner: Aspects of his spiritual world view (3 volumes)
Anthroposophy vol. I: *Rudolf Steiner. Reincarnation and karma. The spiritual nature of the human being. The development of human consciousness.*
Anthroposophy vol. II: *Evolution of the world and humanity. Relationships between the living and the dead. Forces of evil. The modern path of initiation.*
Anthroposophy vol. III: *Life between death and rebirth. The spiritual hierarchies. The philosophical approach to the spirit. The mission of Christ.*

May be ordered from: Rudolf Steiner College Bookstore
9200 Fair Oaks Boulevard
Fair Oaks, CA 95628, USA
Tel: (916) 961-8729 — Fax: (916) 961-3032